CODING ACTIVITIES FOR
MAKING
ANIMATION
AND ART
IN SCRATCH

Adam Furgang

ROSEN
PUBLISHING

For Scratchers Ben and Caleb

Published in 2022 by The Rosen Publishing Group, Inc.
29 East 21st Street, New York, NY 10010

Library of Congress Cataloging-in-Publication Data

Names: Furgang, Adam, author.
Title: Coding activities for making animation and art in Scratch / Adam Furgang.
Description: First edition. | New York, NY : The Rosen Publishing Group, Inc., 2022. | Series: Code creator | Includes bibliographical references and index. | Audience: Grades 7–12.
Identifiers: LCCN 2019010327| ISBN 9781725340930 (library bound) | ISBN 9781725340923 (pbk.)
Subjects: LCSH: Computer animation—Juvenile literature. | Scratch (Computer program language)—Juvenile literature. | Computer programming—Juvenile literature.
Classification: LCC TR897.72.S38 F87 2022 | DDC 006.6/96—dc23
LC record available at https://lccn.loc.gov/2019010327

Manufactured in the United States of America

Some of the images in this book illustrate individuals who are models. The depictions do not imply actual situations or events.

CPSIA Compliance Information: Batch #CSRYA22. For further information contact Rosen Publishing, New York, New York at 1-800-237-9932.

Find us on

Contents

Introduction

While learning a new software language can seem overwhelming, the art and animation activities here will provide a foundation to programming with the free visual programming language called Scratch. Learning to code with a programming language can be an exciting challenge—and also a lot of fun.

Scratch was created as an introductory coding language software. It uses visual colored blocks to program, which makes it easier to remember. The idea of using visual blocks as a programming language was created to help introduce programming concepts to beginner coders of all ages, especially young ones. The different code blocks each have different properties and commands. Stacked together, the blocks create software programs that can run games, animations, and interactive stories. With the right training, Scratch users are capable of making coding decisions that bring artistic animated creations to life.

To understand the importance of computer software languages such as Scratch, it helps to learn about the history of animation and computers. Animation is a simulation of movement created by

There is no need to be stressed about learning to code animation and art programs. The visual programming language Scratch was designed to help people learn to code.

displaying a quickly changing series of drawings or pictures. The earliest forms of animation were created between the 1600s and the 1800s and used mechanisms like magic lanterns and zoetropes that depicted movement through a series of different pictures that were quickly displayed, one after another.

In 1937, Walt Disney released the first hand-drawn, feature-length animated film: *Snow White and the Seven Dwarfs*. After its release, traditional hand-drawn animation became very popular and was increasingly used for animated films and TV cartoons.

The next major advance in animation came alongside improvements in computer technology in the 1970s and 1980s. As computers became faster and smaller, computer software became a very important tool for the creation of various forms of media, such as video games, television shows, and films—all of which use art and animation. Soon, segments of CGI (computer-generated imagery) were being used in live action films such as *TRON* in 1982. In 1983, the Canadian animated film *Rock & Rule* became the first traditionally animated film to use segments of CGI in parts of the film.

Another big step forward in the computer animation industry came in 1995, when the computer animation company Pixar released

As computer technology improved in the 1980s, personal computers became common in homes and businesses. Animators were immediately drawn to these machines.

Toy Story, the first feature-length computer-animated film. After *Toy Story's* success, many more computer-animated films were produced. Today, concept art, character art, and drawings are still done by hand, but computers are often used as tools to draw on and to aid with movement, coloring, timing, lighting, shading, texture, and more. Contemporary computer animation is also used for special effects in live-action movies.

This is where Scratch comes in. This software suite can be used to make all kinds of interesting, engaging content—including art and animation. The activities in this resource will make use of Scratch 3.0, which was released on January 2, 2019. Using Scratch requires a tablet, laptop, or desktop computer. Scratch is free to download and can be found at the website https://scratch.mit.edu.

Today, the ability to program computers is being taught in schools. Scratch is free to use and easy to understand, making learning to program a fun experience.

The software can be either used in your browser—with no downloading necessary—or it can be downloaded for use on a desktop, no browser required. The link for the downloaded version is https://scratch.mit.edu/download. Scratch currently supports both Windows and macOS.

To save Scratch projects, it is a good idea to create a personal Scratch account. Find the Join Scratch tab at the top of the browser screen and follow the steps by creating a username and password and filling out some basic information, such as an email address and your date of birth. Be sure to keep track of your Scratch username and password, as you will need them to log into your account in the future. Once set up, there are additional customization options for your Scratch profile, but none of that will be necessary to complete these activities.

Activity 1

Scratching the Surface: Move the Sprite

From the Scratch website's homepage, click the Create tab. (Or simply run the desktop application if you downloaded the program.)

After clicking Create, the Scratch Project Editor launches. Before getting started, it is a good idea to become familiar with the different areas of the Project Editor.

Starting from the top left: the Scratch logo will exit the Project Editor and return to the homepage. (In the desktop version of Scratch, that button is not clickable.) To the right of the Scratch home button, there is a globe icon for selecting the language. Next, there is File, with a drop-down options list: New, Save now, Save as a copy, Load from your computer, and Save to your computer. These options are used to create new Scratch programs, save a current program, or load an older program.

Next is Edit, with the drop-down options list: Restore and Turn on Turbo Mode. Restore can sometimes be helpful; it is essentially an "undo" button. Turbo Mode helps the program run faster, although it will not be needed for these activities. Next is Tutorials, with a light bulb icon, where there are many great instructional videos to help with creating various projects in Scratch.

To the right of the Tutorials tab is a field with the word "Untitled." This is where Scratch projects are named. This first project can be named Activity1.

Below the Scratch menu are several different areas. On the left are three tabs for creating Code, Costumes, and Sounds. On the right is the stage with a sprite called Scratch Cat. A sprite is any object in Scratch that can be programmed to move or perform an action. The stage is where programmed projects will be seen. Below the stage are the sprite list and the backdrops areas. Use these to choose sprites or backdrops.

On the left of the Scratch screen is the Code tab, which contains many different code blocks. Each code block is grouped and color coded according to its function. Blue code blocks, for example, control motion. Try clicking on the different code block circles on the left to see the many different code block types. To the right of the code blocks is an empty code area where the code blocks can be dragged and snapped together to create a program.

Clicking the Costumes tab opens the costume area, in which it is possible to draw custom Sprites or choose existing ones.

The last tab is the Sounds tab. This can be used to load many different premade sounds or record new ones. It is here that the length, volume, and duration of sounds can be configured.

The Scratch Project Editor may seem complex, but with practice, it quickly becomes familiar and easy to use. The goal of this first activity is to use code blocks from the Code tab to control the Scratch Cat sprite on the stage.

Go to the Code tab and scroll down to the yellow Events code blocks. Find the yellow "when clicked" block with a green flag in it and drag it to the code area. This tells the program to start when the green flag is pressed. This green flag—used to start programs in Scratch—is located above the stage; there is also a red stop sign next to the flag, which is used to stop the program.

Code blocks get attached to one another from the top down. The order in which the code block commands are stacked is the order in which the actions will occur.

Next, find the blue "move 10 steps" Motion block and attach it below the "when clicked" block in the open space. Any block with a white field indicates a variable that can be changed. Variables can use decimal points, such as .25, as well as negative numbers, such as –23.

Add an orange "wait 1 second" Control block, a blue "turn clockwise 15 degrees" Motion block, an orange "wait 1 second" Control block, a purple "say Hello! for 2 seconds" block, a blue "move 10 steps" Motion block and add a negative sign before the 10. Then, add another orange "wait 1 second" Control block, and finally a blue "turn counterclockwise 15 degrees" Motion block.

In the purple "say Hello! for 2 seconds" block, change the text to: "Hello world … Let's make some art and animation" and the duration to 4 seconds.

With all that code in place, click the green flag and watch the Scratch Cat sprite as your very first Scratch animation springs to life. Use the red stop sign to stop it at any time.

Try changing the sprite message and the duration or distance of the code blocks and see what the results are. You can also try making a new project and experimenting with all the various tools available. The best thing about Scratch is that mistakes do not mean much—it is easy to just delete a project and start a new one if things do not work out perfectly the first time.

Activity 2

Let's Get Drawing: Becoming a Scratcher

Anyone who creates projects with Scratch is called a Scratcher. A user with a new account is listed as a New Scratcher. After creating and sharing several projects, that label changes to simply Scratcher. It is important to always be respectful with the projects you create and share. Scratch has always been a free program and an open community with many great Scratchers creating and sharing unique and interesting projects. Every user needs to make sure to keep up the strong community values that make the program so special.

Inside the Project Editor, sprites are the main elements that get used as the subject matter for projects. Scratch has many great ready-to-use sprites available in the Sprite Library. To access the Sprite Library, go to the Sprite List located below the stage. Sprite Cat will be listed there as Sprite1. At the bottom left is a blue cat icon with a + symbol. Click the icon to: Choose a Sprite, Paint, Surprise, or Upload a Sprite. Click the magnifying glass icon and click Choose a Sprite. This brings up the Sprite Library; from here, it is possible to add any of these premade sprites to the stage. Scroll around for a bit, then return to the main screen.

Without backdrops, animation would be pretty boring. Choosing or creating a backdrop is just as easy as creating a sprite. Just next to the Sprite List is the backdrops stage. Use the Choose a Backdrop icon the same way you use the Choose a Sprite icon to select from many ready-to-use backdrops, paint a custom backdrop, or upload a backdrop.

For now, return to the Sprite Library. Explore all the sprites by scrolling up and down the list or clicking the categories. Moving the mouse over certain sprites will cause them to move, or animate. Sprites that move have several costumes; these costumes are just different pictures of a sprite in a different position, shape, or color. These come in handy for making a sprite move realistically.

Once you find a sprite you like, click on it. The screen will change back to the Scratch Project Editor and the new sprite will appear on the stage along with Sprite Cat. The new sprite will also appear on the Sprite List next to Sprite1.

Even though there are many great sprites to choose from, it is also possible to create a customized sprite. In the Choose a Sprite menu, select the Paint option, which will open the Paint Editor. The Paint Editor has many tools and features to help create sprites or backdrops for any kind of Scratch project. Take some time to use the Paint

Editor to create a brand-new sprite. Mistakes can easily be fixed using the undo and redo arrows at the top of the Paint Editor.

Scratch 3.0 has two different ways to draw: bitmap and vector graphics. Bitmap graphics use individual pixels to create an image. Digital cameras also use pixels to create photos. If you create a bitmap sprite in Scratch, the Paint Editor tools generate the art with pixels.

The other drawing mode in Scratch is called vector graphics. Vector is the default drawing mode in Scratch 3.0. Vector mode uses instructions to create shapes, rather than pixels. Using the vector drawing mode, create a simple face using the brush tool or the circle tool. To choose a new color, click on the Fill color chooser above the drawing area. Use the sliders to change the color, saturation, and brightness. Use the paint bucket fill tool to fill in a shape with the selected color. The select tool can be used to select a shape and then change its dimensions, color, outline color, outline width, and orientation.

Once you have created a custom sprite, it can be imported onto the stage just like any of the premade ones from the Sprite Library. It can then be animated and manipulated. For an extra project, try drawing a sprite or a backdrop on paper and importing it into Scratch with the use of a digital camera. To do this, use the Upload Sprite or Upload Backdrop icons to import artwork or a digital image.

Activity 3

Let's Get Moving: Looping Animated Movement

Start this activity off by setting the stage with a single sprite and a single backdrop. These can be anything, so long as there is one of each.

Inside the stage panel, use the mouse to click on the sprite and move it to where you would like it to start on the backdrop. To make the sprite move and talk, it is time to return to code blocks. Click the Code tab on the left and start by placing a yellow "when clicked" block in the code area. Now choose a blue "move 10 steps" block and attach it. Change the number to 25. Next, click on the purple Looks code blocks. These can be used to add dialogue bubbles (such as the "Hello world" used earlier), switch to different costumes or backdrops, and change size and color. For now, choose the "think Hmm ... for 2 seconds" block and attach it. Add another "move" block (the distance can be anything) and then add a purple "say Hello! for 2 seconds" block. Click the green flag to see what happens.

In Scratch, the stage and Paint Editor both use a 480 x 360 pixel grid with x (horizontal) and y (vertical) coordinates for a sprite's axis, placement, and movement. Coordinates are presented like this: (x-value, y-value). Here are some important things to know:

- Make sure sprites are located at the center of the Paint Editor. This will center the sprite's coordinates (0, 0), which is helpful for programming the sprite using the x and y grid coordinates in the stage view. A sprite placed off-center on the Paint Editor will have an off-center axis, regardless of where it is placed on the stage.
- The center of the stage is (0, 0).
- The upper right-hand corner of the stage is (240, 180).
- The upper left-hand corner of the stage is (-240, 180).
- The bottom right-hand corner of the stage is (240, -180).
- The bottom left-hand corner of the stage is (-240, -180).

To identify the coordinates of a sprite on any point on the stage, simply select the sprite and look at the x and y coordinates below the stage and above the sprite list. There is a blue "go to x:0 y:0" code block to program in x and y coordinates to get a sprite to move anywhere on the stage.

The Paint Editor is where you will be creating art for your animated programs. The stage is where you will see your programs come to life when you run them.

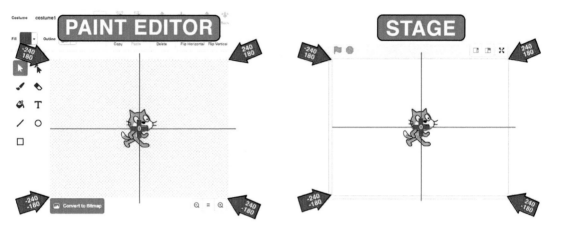

With all that in place, it is time to make some choices. Where should the sprite move? What should the sprite say or think? These are questions whose answers are creative programming choices. Deciding how far to move a sprite and what they should be doing is the first step in creating a real animation.

Scratch has many code blocks. Here are a few to try with this activity:

- Blue "glide 1 secs t x: 0 y: 0." Use this block to program the sprite to move at different speeds to any coordinates on the stage.

- Orange "wait 1 second." Use this block to program pauses; this is helpful to slow down the action for pacing.
- Orange "repeat 10." Place any block, or group of programmed blocks, into a "repeat 10" block to get a sprite to repeat a program for a specific amount.

After trying those blocks out, experiment a little more with combinations of these basic blocks.

Activity 4

Blast Off! Animation with Multiple Sprites

In nearly all animated movies—large or small—there are often several characters moving on the screen at once with a changing background behind them. To accomplish a scene with several moving characters or elements, each needs to be sketched and thought out in advance, all while taking the background into consideration.

In this activity, click Choose a Backdrop and import one that looks like outer space; there is a Space filter in the library. Choose one as the backdrop of this project. This backdrop can always be changed at a later time.

Next, use the Paint Editor to create a rocket ship. It may be helpful to sketch out a design on paper before trying it out in Scratch. Use the paintbrush tool and the shape tools to get started. To create more complex shapes, use the reshape tool to add or remove vector points on figures. For example, to make a triangle, use the rectangle tool and draw a rectangle. Then, use the reshape tool—which looks like a mouse cursor with a circle at the point—and double-click on a vector point to remove it. To add a point, click on any place on a line where it should be added. Use the select tool to change the size of a shape. Take some time to play with the tools to see what can be done.

With this new experience, use the shapes and shaping tools to create a rocket ship sprite. If there are many shapes that are components of a single sprite, they can be grouped together using the Group tool. To select all the shapes to be grouped, click and drag the select tool around a sprite. Once all the shapes have been selected, click the Group tool. Now, the sprite with many shapes can be moved around in the Paint Editor all at once.

By creating different shapes in the Paint Editor, it will be easy to combine shapes to make a complex piece of art, like this rocket ship.

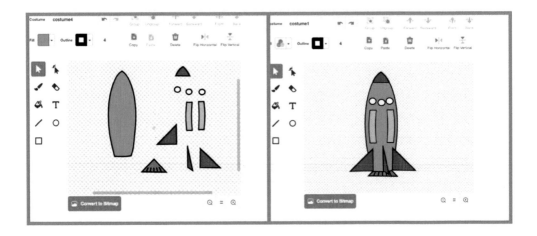

With the new rocket ship sprite created, right-click on it in the sprite list. This will bring up an option to duplicate the sprite. Make two copies of the sprite and give them each a different name. Change the colors of the other rocket ship sprites

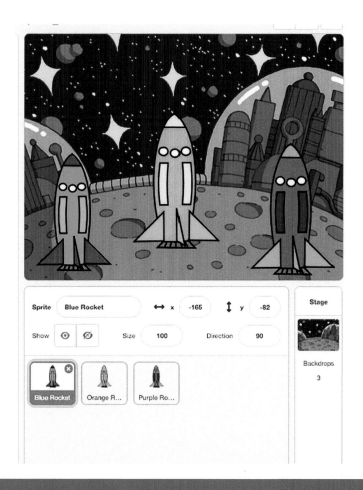

Scratch makes it easy to duplicate sprites and change their colors. Adding a background will help you program complex animation with multiple elements.

so they each look different from one another. If a sprite needs to be resized, select it in the Paint Editor and make it bigger or smaller. Be sure to leave each sprite centered in the Paint Editor.

Now that there are three rocket ship sprites, it is time for blastoff. Choose the first rocket ship and click the Code tab. Add the following code blocks:

- "when clicked"
- "Go to x: -165 y: -82"
- "wait 3 seconds"
- "Glide 3 secs to x: -164 y: 235"

Repeat these steps for the other two rocket ships, but be sure to enter different Go to and Glide coordinates for each sprite. To find the starting Go to (x, y) coordinates, place the rocket ship on the stage where you want it to start. Its (x, y) grid coordinates on the stage are listed below in the Sprite List. To determine where you want the rocket ship to end, simply move it to the desired end position on the stage and copy the (x, y) grid coordinates listed in the sprite area into the "Glide 3 secs to" code block. Make sure to do this for each rocket ship. To watch the full program once each rocket has its own set of instructions, click the green flag.

Activity 5

A Good Place to Land: Adding Dialogue

Advanced animation can have several moving elements all happening at the same time. The addition of dialogue to a scene can help to tell a story and make the scene exciting. Both are equally important in a good animation.

This activity will use the orange "forever" code block. The forever code block has a top and bottom section so that any segment of connected code blocks can be placed inside this. Code blocks placed inside a forever code block will repeat their programming forever—or until the red stop sign icon is clicked.

The goal here is to program a flying rocket ship that is trying to land on a constantly spinning planet. Start off by creating a new rocket ship sprite or reuse one from the previous activity. To reuse a sprite from another Scratch program, open that program and drag the sprite, or program code, into the Backpack section at the bottom of the Scratch screen. Sprites and code block programs can be stored there and reused across multiple programs.

However, always be sure to save one program before closing it and opening another.

To program the new rocket ship sprite for this activity, attach the following code blocks together:

- "when clicked"
- "forever" (place all the following code blocks inside the forever block)
- "glide 1 secs to random position"
- "turn counterclockwise 35 degrees"
- "say 'I need to find a good spot to land' for 3 seconds"
- "wait 1 second"
- "glide 1 sec to random position"
- "turn counterclockwise 35 degrees"
- "say 'This is going to be tricky' for 3 seconds"
- "wait 1 second"

With that in place, it is time to add a spinning planet. Choose the Galaxy, Nebula, or Stars backdrop and add it to the stage. Now, start creating an alien planet. Go to the Paint Editor and use the circle tool to make a planet. Get creative and add multicolored swirls, stripes, or craters to it and change the colors around as well. Once it is finished, group it all together and center it on the Paint Editor.

To program the alien planet to spin clockwise, attach the following code blocks together:

- "when clicked"
- "forever" (place all the following code blocks inside the forever block)
- "wait .1 second"
- "turn clockwise 15 degrees"

Now click the green flag and run the program. The alien planet will spin clockwise while the rocket ship continually moves around randomly, looking for a place to land. As the rocket ship pauses, dialogue will pop up and give the scene a never-ending narrative for viewers to follow.

Art that Pops: Dynamic Art

Just as technology changes and evolves, so does art and the way it is created and presented. Art has traditionally been painted on canvas using paint. In the 1960s, pop artist Andy Warhol began screen-printing photos onto canvas. Contemporary artists have begun creating art digitally on computers, tablets, and mobile phones. In 2014, artist David Hockney exhibited artworks he created on an iPad painting app at the de Young Museum in San Francisco, California. Using computers to create art can be a lot of fun.

In this activity, Scratch will be used to create a dynamic pop art piece that changes images and colors in succession. Each piece of art created this way should look slightly different. To start off, gather three to five pieces of art or photo collages to work with. These can be anything. For example, you could import a series of pictures of a friend, taken with a digital camera, into Scratch. The subject could make different faces or expressions in each picture. These different photos will be used to create a collage; aim for about ten pictures per collage, and create at least three collages.

Once all the photos are in place, there are many ways to turn them into dynamic pop art. The images need to be grouped or collaged together in rows and columns to make a grid. There are many free image-editing websites available for making collages like this. Another simple way to collage the photos together in a grid is to place the photo icons next to one another on the computer and take a screen shot of their arrangement. If necessary, research how to make a screen shot on your computer or mobile device.

Using actual photos is not necessary for this activity, however. It will also work with art created in Scratch or drawn by hand. In either case, be sure to draw or paint several pieces of art for this activity. If drawing art by hand, import the images by photographing them and uploading them into Scratch.

Once the artwork is arranged into a grid pattern, there are several ways to change the colors or images using Scratch. The simplest way is to start with a single sprite. Choose Upload Sprite from the sprite list and import a single photo collage or artwork into Scratch. Start with a yellow "when clicked" code block. Then add an orange "forever" code block. End by placing a purple "change color effect by 25" code block inside the forever block.

Click the green flag to see the results. The purple "change color effect" code block shifts the colors of any sprite; change the number to speed up or slow down the color changes.

To incorporate multiple collages or art pieces into one dynamic piece, upload each image as a separate costume for a single sprite. To do this, upload a single photo collage or artwork as a new sprite. Next, go to the Costumes tab for that sprite and click Upload Costume. Add each additional photo collage or artwork as a new costume. It is also possible to use the Paint option to create alternate costumes within Scratch. Once all the costumes have been set, attach the following code:

- Start with a yellow "when clicked" code block.
- Add 1 orange "forever" code block.
- Insert an orange "wait 1 second" code block and a purple "next costume" code block into the "forever" code block. Change the number on the orange "wait 1 second" code block to .2 to speed up the change between costumes. Using decimal points allows for finer control over programming time duration.
- End by clicking the green flag to see the photo collage or artwork change from one variation to the next.

Try using the "change color effect" code block and the "next costume" code block in combination to see different results. Stack purple "switch costume to" code blocks to pick which costume comes next. Add an orange "wait 1 second" code block—with varying numbers—to change the speed.

Sprightly Sprites: Advanced Sprite Drawing

Creating sprites with multiple costumes allows for changes or animated movement when Scratch is programmed to change a sprite's costume. A sprite's costume can be programmed to change once or multiple times in rapid succession allowing for animated movement. Scratch also allows for color changes to be programmed into animation.

Scratch 3.0 has two different ways to draw sprites: bitmap and vector. This activity will focus on the latter. This is because using the vector drawing method will allow for the creation of a single sprite with multiple parts. A sprite made of multiple parts can be duplicated into a new costume with each part moved slightly. This will allow for more advanced animation of a sprite.

To create a sprite character, start by sketching out some ideas on paper. Use these early sketches as a guide for drawing a new sprite within Scratch.

Use the various drawing and shape tools in the Paint Editor to create the different parts of a new sprite. Create a head with a mouth, eyes, mouth, and nose. When the head is finished, group all the parts together by selecting it all with the Select tool. Then click the Group button to group those parts. This will make it easier to reposition multiple sprite parts. Next, make the body with separate arms and legs. Once all the parts are created, group them together individually and then group the entire sprite character together.

Once this multipart sprite has been created, duplicate the sprite as a new costume. Each new

Separate shapes created in the Paint Editor can be moved separately to bring an animated character to life. In Scratch, each variation of a single sprite is referred to as a costume.

costume can then be ungrouped and the various parts moved. Different costumes of the same character in different positions will allow you to use the purple "switch costume to" blocks to change a sprite's position, or—if many costumes are created—animate the sprite.

Here are some of the advanced things that are possible with the Paint Editor's vector tools:

- Make shapes that can be altered with points
- Draw with the brush, line, circle, or rectangle tools
- Add or delete anchor points with the reshape tool; click to add an anchor point, double-click to delete an anchor point
- Use the paint bucket tool to fill in shapes
- Outline shapes with different colors or widths
- Use the Fill and Outline buttons to choose colors
- Group shapes using the select tool and the Group button
- Ungroup shapes by selecting them and clicking the Ungroup button
- Duplicate shapes by using the Copy and Paste buttons
- Use the Flip Horizontal or Flip Vertical buttons to change an object's orientation along an axis
- Move objects in front or behind each other using the Forward, Backward, Front, and Back buttons
- Add text to a sprite or make a text sprite with the text tool

Try creating multiple costumes of a single sprite in various positions and animating the sprite using the purple "switch costume to" or "next costume" blocks. Use at least five directions from this bulleted list to make the animation as smooth as possible.

Activity 8

For Comic Effects: Sprite Animation Effects

Comics and animation often make use of visual graphic effects to express movement or action. Japanese animation and comics (called anime and manga, respectively) have a very unique style and have been influential in the United States and the rest of the world. This activity will create anime- and manga-style visual effects. These visual effects can be used to enhance Scratch animation and art projects and make them more exciting to view.

One of the most important tools for this activity will be the ability to create a graphic animation effect sprite with multiple costumes, which can then be animated and programmed to change between the costumes. These visual aids are used in conjunction with a sprite character or objects to create more dynamic art or animation.

To start off, search around online for examples of comic action effects, manga effects, and anime effects. The image results will display many types of dynamic effects, such as smoke, fire, water, ice, lightning, energy, and explosions. Other comic effects that use text words are also widely available online. Use these results as inspiration and then sketch out some ideas for similar effects in Scratch.

Use the various Paint Editor vector tools to create an effect sprite. This sprite will have multiple costumes that will change in shape, size, and color. Create a series of different costumes for the effects sprite. Consider the size of the effects sprite that the effect starts with. For example, an explosion effects sprite should start small and each additional

You can create your own visual graphic effects shapes by hand, in an art software program, or by using the Paint Editor in Scratch.

costume should be larger and larger. A fire effects sprite could have costumes that are flipped horizontally so the fire appears to be flickering back and forth as the sprite costumes change. Each additional costume for an effect should work to make the animation look somewhat realistic.

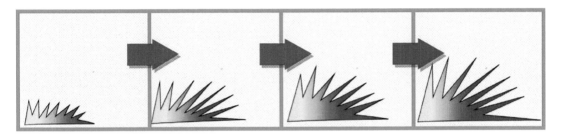

Duplicating a sprite and altering its shape will allow you to create different costumes. These can be programmed to appear in sequence with purple "switch costume to" blocks.

After creating a shape with the Paint Editor, here are some tricks to help alter it into a more complex shape for the animation:

- Move, rotate, or resize a shape with the select tool
- Add or delete anchor points to any shape with the reshape tool
- Use the reshape tool to move anchor points to make a new shape

- Control the shape of a line between two anchor points with the anchor point control handles
- Use the Curved or Pointed buttons when using the reshape tool to round out or point the edges of a shape
- Use the text tool to type words. Text can be resized and distorted with the select tool, but it cannot be manipulated with anchor points like shapes can

The effects sprite with multiple costumes has been created. It is time to begin programming. Each costume—and there should be several—should be named Costume1, Costume2, and so on. Add these blocks of code to the base sprite:

- Start with a yellow "when clicked" block.
- Add an orange "repeat 10" block. Change the number to 1.
- Add a purple "switch costume to" block inside the previous block.
- Add an orange "wait 1 second" block and change the number to .2.
- Add an additional "switch costume to" block and "wait 1 second" block after each one; there should be one switch for each costume.

With this in place, there should be a purple "switch costume to" block for each costume the effect sprite has. Start at the top and select each costume and change each purple "switch costume to" block to Costume1, Costume2, and so on—make sure to go in order. Click the green flag to run the program and the effects sprite animation should play as each costume changes quickly to the next.

To have the effects sprite animation end and disappear, add a blank costume to the bottom of the costumes. Do this by duplicating the last costume in the costume list and deleting the image from it. Then add an additional "switch costume to" block and "wait 1 second" block to the bottom of the program. The animation will play and then disappear now.

Change the time duration of the "repeat" and "wait" code blocks to get different results. Create a backdrop with different costumes and program it to change backdrops. Combine a character sprite along with an action effects sprite and a background to create a dynamic visual image or scene. All of these things will make the animation exciting.

Activity 9

Creating Short Circuits: Digital Comic Book

Comic strips, comic books, and graphic novels tell a story when read from panel to panel and page to page. Digital comics can use programming to switch from one comic panel to the next.

That will be the object of this activity: creating a digital comic with several panels that change from one piece of artwork to the next. To get inspiration, look at comic books, comic strips in the newspaper, or search online for popular comics. Notice how comic panels each have different pictures and use word bubbles to help tell a story.

With that research out of the way, start brainstorming about an idea for an original comic. It should have around five to ten panels. Your comic can be drawn entirely by hand (and then imported into Scratch using a digital camera) or created entirely in Scratch. If drawn by hand and imported, keep in mind that each comic panel will need to be a separately uploaded image.

If created in Scratch, each new comic panel should be a new costume for a single sprite. Choose or create a backdrop for the project. If the comic needs different backdrops for different panels, make any additional backdrops into costumes for the starting backdrop. Name and number all costumes for sprites and backdrops. Naming and numbering sprite costumes helps make programming in Scratch easier when switching from costume to costume.

Once the completed comic panels are ready as a single sprite with different costumes, the programming can be applied. Only three different code blocks are needed to program this activity. Start with a yellow "when clicked" code block. Add an orange "wait 1 second" code block. Then add a "switch costume to" code block and a "wait 1 second" code block for each comic panel that will appear in your digital comic. To create word bubbles in Scratch, program them using purple "say" code blocks and change the field to contain the panel's text.

Change the first "switch costume to" code block to Costume1. Continue down the program, changing each "switch costume to" code block to the next costume in the sequence. Then click the green flag icon.

Comic Panel 1   Comic Panel 2   Comic Panel 3   Comic Panel 4

A digital comic that tells a story can be created by programming Scratch to use backgrounds, sprites, multiple costumes, and text, all at the same time.

Timing for a printed comic is not necessary; the person reading each panel can take as much time as they need before continuing on. With a programmed digital comic, however, it is important to program in the timing to give the reader enough time to read the panel before the picture changes. When watching this program play, check how long it takes to read each panel and make a note of it. Some panels may need to change after one second, while others require several seconds to read. Once you have observed how long each comic panel should appear to be easily read, change the seconds on the orange "wait 1 second" code block directly below the corresponding purple "switch costume to" code block. Run the program again to see how the timing works and make adjustments to have a panel appear longer or shorter if needed.

Try to add in purple "say" or "think" code blocks to generate comic dialogue in Scratch. Additionally, if you would like to introduce movement into your digital Scratch comic, create additional sprites with additional costumes and program them each separately. This will make the animation run smoothly and look great.

Activity 10

Sound Bytes: Advanced Sprite Conversation

Multiple characters that interact with one another, often with sound, are common in animation. This final activity will bring everything together to create an animated short scene with two different sprites. The characters created here will switch costumes and interact with one another while having a conversation. This activity will also make use of timed word bubbles between two interacting sprites as well as the addition of recorded sounds at the end.

Check out this example of a Scratch-made animated short titled "Dino Conversation." Set up the stage by adding Dinosaur1 and Dinosaur2 sprite and setting the backdrop to Forest. Then, place the Dinosaur1 sprite on the bottom right corner and the Dinosaur2 sprite on the bottom left. Each of these dinosaurs will get their own code blocks. For Dinosaur2:

- "When clicked"
- "switch costume to dinosaur2-a"

- "go to x: -147 y: -95"
- "move 10 steps"
- "wait 4 seconds"
- "move 10 steps"
- "say "Hello Brutus. How are you?" for 3 seconds"
- "wait 10 seconds"
- "switch costume to dinosaur2-b"
- "say "Nope. What happened to him?" for 4 seconds"
- "switch costume to dinosaur2-c"
- "wait 5 seconds"
- "think "Hmmm...""
- "switch costume to dinosaur2-d"
- "say "That's too bad. Did he get in trouble?" for 2 seconds"
- "switch costume to dinosaur2-a"
- "wait 5 seconds"
- "think "Hmmm...""
- "wait 1 second"
- "say "Hahahahaha!" for 3 seconds"

For Dinosaur1:
- "When clicked"
- "switch costume to dinosaur1-a"
- "go to x: 134 y: -75"
- "move -10 steps"
- "wait 1 second"

- "Say "Hello Red!" for 2 seconds"
- "move -5 steps"
- "wait 5 seconds"
- "Say "I'm doing great." for 2 seconds"
- "Think "Hmmm..." for 2 seconds"
- "Say "Did you hear what happened to Rex?" for 4 seconds"
- "switch costume to dinosaur1-b"
- "wait 1 second"
- "switch costume to dinosaur1-c"
- "wait 4 seconds"
- "switch costume to dinosaur1-d"
- "Move -5 steps"
- "Say "His mom said he was punished." for 2 seconds"
- "switch costume to dinosaur1-a"
- "wait 8 seconds"
- "Say "Yes. He ate his dessert without asking!" for 2 seconds"

This example short demonstrates how animators have to be able to think about both characters at once—the code for Dinosaur1 would not make sense without the code for Dinosaur2, and vice versa. It is important to keep in mind the timing and placement of the sprites in any animation.

With this example in mind, it is time to make your own original animated short. The way to start off is to write a short screenplay with dialogue for two characters. You can use premade sprites from Scratch or create your own with the Paint Editor. Make sure to pick sprites that have several costumes, such as the Dinosaur1 and Dinosaur2 sprites. A custom sprite will also need multiple costumes. Now, create or pick a backdrop that will fit into the screenplay.

With those in place, begin to program the animated short. There are two ways to do this: programming the sprites one at a time or bouncing back and forth between them. Whichever method you use, make sure that the speech bubbles and movements line up; sprites should not be talking over each other, for example. Test the timing of the program as it moves along. By doing this, it will be easy to tell when and where mistakes are happening. Once all the programming is done and the timings line up, run the program to watch the animation play out.

To add a little more creativity to the project, consider adding sound. For an original animation, like this is, it will be necessary to record custom dialogue. To do this, click on the Sounds tab. Under the Sounds tab are options to Choose a Sound, Record, Surprise, and Upload Sound. Click Record to open the Record Sound feature. Click the red Record button to record a clip. Once it has been recorded, there are several options: trim, play, re-record, and save. Experiment with these options until reaching a sound that works for your animation, then click Save. This sound can—and should—be renamed to something that makes sense for your screenplay (Dialogue1, for example). Record a new sound for each purple "say" block of existing dialogue for the sprites in your animation.

The magenta Sound code blocks are used to program sounds. To add recorded dialogue to an existing sprite program, create a new program alongside the existing one. This is what the "Dino Conversation" short looks like with custom dialogue sound effects:

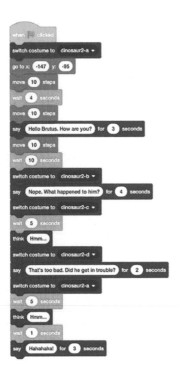

```
when clicked
switch costume to  dinosaur1-a ▼
go to x: 134  y: -75
move -10 steps
wait 1 seconds
say Hello Red!  for 2 seconds
move -5 steps
wait 5 seconds
say I'm doing great.  for 2 seconds
think Hmm...  for 2 seconds
say Did you hear what happend to Rex?  for 4 seconds
switch costume to  dinosaur1-b ▼
wait 1 seconds
switch costume to  dinosaur1-c ▼
wait 4 seconds
switch costume to  dinosaur1-d ▼
move -5 steps
say His mom said he was punished.  for 2 seconds
switch costume to  dinosaur1-a ▼
wait 8 seconds
say Yes. He ate his dessert without asking!  for 2 seconds
```

```
when clicked
wait 1 seconds
play sound  helo red ▼  until done
wait 6 seconds
play sound  great ▼  until done
wait 1 seconds
play sound  hmmm...did you hear ▼  until done
wait 7 seconds
play sound  punished ▼  until done
wait 8 seconds
play sound  Dessert without asking ▼  until done
```

Advanced sprite programming with sounds can get complicated. Take your time to create a separate program for sound alongside the animation program for a single sprite.

Try adding in some dialogue and sound effects to your original animation in a similar way. Again, remember to test the timing to make sure the sprites are not talking over each other or moving where they should not be. Adjust the wait times as necessary.

Career Connections

When considering a career in art and animation, computer programming may not spring to mind as an essential skill for success. Traditional animation and contemporary computer programming skills may seem incompatible—but, in fact, they are often used together. The credits for any film or video game contain hundreds of names; many of these people are computer animators who use software

Using Scratch to create programs is the first step on the path to learning more complex computer languages that can lead to a career in art and animation programming.

programs to create animations for media projects of all kinds. Careers in programming are also closely linked to animation. A video game programmer is someone who programs the code a video game uses to run. A video game designer will work closely with programmers and animators and will possess skills in both areas. The overlap between art, animation, and computer programming is one essential part of creating video games that both look good and function correctly.

In addition to creating art and animations, computer animators also need to be familiar with continually changing computer programs that help them create. Computer animation programmers often create the actual software programs that computer animators use. Because of this, they must work closely with one another. Understanding how computer software languages work and are used—even if not using them directly—is an asset in many careers.

This intersection of computer science and art and animation produces a new creative skill set that often combines both professions. Because computer programming has become important in nearly every industry, the need for more people to learn computer science has grown. This has given rise to simple approaches in teaching computer programming. Scratch was invented to teach programming concepts to both young people and beginners.

Mitchel Resnick, a professor of learning research at the Massachusetts Institute of Technology (MIT) Media Lab, worked to develop the first desktop-based version of Scratch in 2003. The drag-and-drop, block-based visual system for the Scratch programming language was inspired by construction toys. These toys—and the language of Scratch—fit together perfectly to form a complete whole. The concept of adding smaller pieces up to create something larger is the very foundation of computer programming, and it is a valuable skill to learn.

In a 2007 interview with Stephanie Schorow of MIT News, Resnick said, "Until now, only expert programmers could make interactive creations for the Web. Scratch opens the gates for everyone ... As kids work on Scratch projects, they learn to think creatively and solve problems systematically—skills that are critical to success in the 21st century." This statement—now well over a decade old—has never been more true. The demands of the modern world require professionals who are comfortable and confident with computers, and Scratch is a great gateway to more advanced programming.

The name Scratch was taken from the remix techniques used by hip-hop disc jockeys who "scratch" several records back and forth and create new music from old music. This is how the program is intended to be used. The MIT-hosted Scratch website makes it easy for users to view existing Scratch projects as well as share their own. There is a huge and constantly growing community of Scratchers who are more than willing to share their experiences and expertise.

Starting with Scratch makes it easier to grasp more complex, syntax-based programming languages, such as Java and Python. With the integration of computer technology into many different fields of interest, having a basic understanding of how computers are programmed and work will be a plus for anyone looking for work in almost any professional field or industry, even those not traditionally associated with computers.

Today, technology is essential in every area of daily life, and across so many careers, and computers have become extremely common. Using Scratch as an introductory stepping-stone will aid anyone wishing to learn computer programming while also starting a career path as an artist or animator off on the right foot.

Glossary

animator Someone who creates animations from art, drawing, or computer wireframe models.

anime A stylized and iconic form of animation that originated in Japan.

backdrop A background in Scratch that sits behind the sprites; it can be created, chosen in the Backdrop Library, or uploaded.

bitmap A visual image or text on a computer screen that is made up of bits or pixels of information.

code A set of instructions used by a computer or software that allows it to run or perform a variety of tasks.

collage An art technique that takes fragments or clippings of images from different, often unrelated, sources and recomposes them together to form a new image or artwork.

coordinates A representation with numbers that describes a specific location on a line, space, or location.

icon An image or picture on a computer screen that represents a file, command, or set of instructions.

manga A stylized form of graphic novels and comic books created in Japan that use pictures to tell stories.

mobile device A portable computer, typically a cellular phone or tablet.

pop art An art movement that uses modern popular culture and the mass media as the basis for its images.

programmer A person who uses coding languages to write computer programs.

resolution The amount of horizontal and vertical pixel detail being displayed on a digital screen.

screenplay The script from a film or television show that also includes the actions and scene settings.

software Programs and operating system instructions that run computers and applications.

sprite Any element, figure, or object in Scratch that moves; it can be created, chosen in the Sprite Library, or uploaded.

syntax A set of rules in a computer language that define how a program's combinations of symbols should be structured.

vector A graphic image or text on a computer screen that is made up of points and lines of information.

video game designer A person who conceptualizes and creates video games, including the mechanics, rules, and the look and feel of the game.

zoetrope An optical mechanical device from the nineteenth century that showed an animated succession of images when spun.

For More Information

Canada Learning Code
129 Spadina Avenue, Unit 501
Toronto, ON M5V2L3
Canada
Website: http://www.canadalearningcode.ca
Facebook: @canadalearningcode
Instagram and Twitter: @learningcode
Canada Learning Code is an organization with a
mission to teach computer coding to all Canadians,
focusing especially on women, girls, people with
disabilities, and indigenous peoples.

Code.org
1501 4th Avenue, Suite 900
Seattle, WA 98101
Website: https://code.org
Facebook: @Code.org
Instagram and Twitter: @codeorg
Code.org is a nonprofit organization that provides
access to computer science learning in schools,
including the program Hour of Code.

Kids & Code
320 Catherine Street
Ottawa, ON K1R5T5
Canada
(613) 862-1412

Website: http://www.kidsandcode.org
Facebook and Twitter: @kidsandcodeorg
Kids & Code is a Canada-based organization
    dedicated to offering classes, workshops, and
    events for kids interested in learning to code.

MIT Media Lab
77 Massachusetts Avenue, E14/E15
Cambridge, MA 02139-4307
(617) 253-5960
Website: https://www.media.mit.edu
Facebook and Instagram: @ mitmedialab
Twitter: @medialab
The MIT Media Lab is the home of many unique
    and exciting projects that combine advanced
    technology with creative thinking. Scratch was
    created here.

Progressive Arts Alliance
3311 Perkins Avenue, Suite 300
Cleveland, OH 44114
(216) 772-4PAA (4722)
Website: http://www.paalive.org
Facebook and Twitter: @progressivearts
Instagram: @ progressive_arts_alliance
The Progressive Arts Alliance helps students and
    families learn about science, algebra, social studies,
    and other topics—and combines these topics
    with art.

Scratch Foundation
7315 Wisconsin Avenue, 4th floor west
Bethesda, MD 20814
Website: https://www.scratchfoundation.org
Facebook: @scratchteam
Instagram: @mitscratchteam
Twitter: @scratch
The parent of the Scratch language and software, the
   Scratch Foundation is dedicated to supporting and
   providing Scratch and creative coding—for free—
   to everyone.

Tynker Coding for Kids
4410 El Camino Real, Suite 104
Los Altos, CA 94022
Website: https://www.tynker.com
Facebook and Twitter: @Gotynker
Instagram: @tynkercoding
Tynker is a company that provides coding and
   technology programs for children interested in
   computer science.

For Further Reading

Ford, Gabriel, Melissa Ford, and Sadie Ford. *Hello Scratch! Learn to Program by Making Arcade Games.* Shelter Island, NY: Manning Publications, 2017.

Furgang, Adam. *Getting to Know Minecraft.* New York, NY: Rosen Publishing, 2019.

Harris, Patricia. *Understanding Coding with Scratch.* New York, NY: Rosen Publishing, 2016.

Marji, Majed. *Learn to Program with Scratch: A Visual Introduction to Programming with Games, Art, Science, and Math.* San Francisco, CA: No Starch Press, 2014.

Rusk, Natalie. *The Official Scratch Coding Cards (Scratch 3.0): Creative Coding Activities for Kids.* 2nd ed. San Francisco, CA: No Starch Press, 2019.

Sweigart, Al. *Scratch Programming Playground: Learn to Program by Making Cool Games.* San Francisco, CA: No Starch Press, 2016.

Woodcock, Jon, and Steve Setford. *Coding in Scratch: Games Workbook: Create Your Own Fun and Easy Computer Games.* New York, NY: DK Publishing, 2016.

Ziter, Rachel. *Coding from Scratch.* North Mankato, MN: Capstone Press, 2018.

Bibliography

Filmsite.org. "Greatest Visual and Special Effects (F/X)—Milestones in Film, 1980–1982." AMC. Retrieved April 2, 2019. https://www.filmsite.org/visualeffects11.html.

Filmsite.org. "Greatest Visual and Special Effects (F/X)—Milestones in Film, 1983–1985." AMC. Retrieved April 2, 2019. https://www.filmsite.org/visualeffects12.html.

Johnson, Phil. "A Method to the Madness: How 13 Programming Languages Got Their Names." IT World, March 19, 2014. https://www.itworld.com/article/2823913/145128-A-method-to-the-madness-How-13-programming-languages-got-their-names.html#slide12.

Maloney, John, et al. "Programming by Choice: Urban Youth Learning Programming with Scratch." Retrieved April 2, 2019. https://web.media.mit.edu/~mres/papers/sigcse-08.pdf.

MAP Systems. "Top 12 Uses of Animation in Various Industries." MAP Systems. Retrieved April 2, 2019. https://mapsystemsindia.com/resources/various-uses-of-animation.html.

Miller, Claire Cain. "IPad Is an Artist's Canvas for David Hockney." *New York Times*, January 10, 2014. https://bits.blogs.nytimes.com/2014/01/10/the-ipad-is-an-artists-canvas-for-david-hockney.

Schorow, Stephanie. "Creating from Scratch: New Software from the MIT Media Lab Unleashes Kids' Creativity Online." MIT News, May 14, 2007. http://news.mit.edu/2007/resnick-scratch.

Scratch. "About Scratch." Scratch.mit.edu. Retrieved April 2, 2019. https://scratch.mit.edu/about.

Scratch. "Animate a Name Cards." Scratch.mit.edu. Retrieved April 2, 2019. https://resources.scratch .mit.edu/www/cards/en/scratch-cards-all.pdf.

Scratch Team. "3 Things to Know About Scratch 3.0." Medium, June 18, 2018. https://medium.com /scratchteam-blog/3-things-to-know-about -scratch-3-0-18ee2f564278.

Software Engineer Insider. "Animation Programmers and Engineers Creative and Passionate." Software Engineer Insider. Retrieved April 2, 2019. https:// www.softwareengineerinsider.com/careers /animation-programmer-engineer.html.

Woodcock, Jon. *Coding Projects in Scratch*. New York, NY: DK Publishing, 2016.

Zeke. "A Quick History of Animation." New York Film Academy, February 26, 2015. https://www.nyfa .edu/student-resources/quick-history-animation.

Index

About the Author

Adam Furgang was first introduced to computers in the 1980s when he played the video games *Load Runner* and *Castle Wolfenstein* on his friend's Apple IIe home computer. In the 1990s, Furgang worked as a web designer at one of the very first social networks, TheGlobe.com. He has continued to work on computers and runs several of his own websites, including a gaming blog, wizardsneverweararmor. com. He lives with his wife and two sons in upstate New York.

Photo Credits

Cover Peshkova/Shutterstock.com; cover, p. 1 (code) © iStockphoto.com/scanrail; p. 5 Odua Images /Shutterstock.com; p. 7 Tom Kelley Archive /Retrofile/Getty Images; p. 8 RIJASOLO/AFP /Getty Images; p. 50 Andia/Universal Images Group/Getty Images; interior pages border design © iStockphoto.com/Akrain.

Design: Matt Cauli; Editor: Siyavush Saidian; Photo Researcher: Sherri Jackson